HIGH DARTMOOR

A shortish guide

Robert Hesketh

Bossiney Books · Launceston

First published 2010 by Bossiney Books Ltd
Langore, Launceston, Cornwall PL15 8LD
www.bossineybooks.com

ISBN 978-1-906474-20-1

The map is by Nick Hawken. All photographs are by the author or publishers.
Printed in Great Britain by R Booth Ltd, Penryn, Cornwall

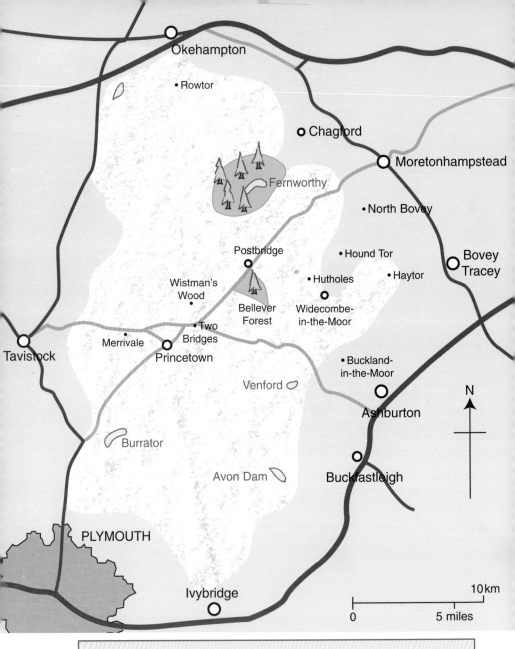

Introduction

Dartmoor has a unique character and is endlessly enjoyable – provided you know where to go and what to look for. This book is designed as a practical guide to high Dartmoor: it is best used alongside the double-sided OS Explorer map OL28.

By 'high Dartmoor' we mean the central area – the land above the cattle grids, much of it unenclosed grazing – which is what immediately attracts most visitors. Dartmoor is often called southern England's largest wilderness, and there are some areas well away from the roads which are truly wild, but even on the high moor the marks of human activity from earlier times are everywhere.

No area of England has more, and more varied, prehistoric remains: stone rows and circles, field boundaries, walled villages, house foundations and hilltop burial chambers. Dartmoor's medieval heritage is equally fascinating, with clapper bridges, pounds, granite churches and church houses, stone crosses and distinctive longhouses as well as the poignantly deserted villages at Hound Tor and Hutholes.

Dartmoor is also an old industrial landscape. Tin streamers and miners left their marks, delving into the earth to follow the precious lodes and cutting leats to drive their simple machinery. Deep mines, quarries, tramways (including the unique Haytor granite tramway), railways and reservoirs came later, but all meld together with the earlier strands of Dartmoor's past to make an extraordinarily rich historic landscape.

Visiting Wistman's Wood calls for a 2km walk each way along a pleasant and generally easy path from the parking space opposite the Two Bridges Hotel, SX609750

The view from Buckland Beacon. It is also the setting for two large stone tablets carved in 1928 with the Ten (or in fact eleven) Command-ments

Natural features

Central Dartmoor's unique physical character, its height and shape, the plants and animals that live there, are chiefly determined by granite, its underlying rock. The 'tors', Dartmoor's rocky hill tops, each have their distinctive profiles – as individual as their names – formed chiefly by horizontal and vertical splitting. These planes of weakness have been opened further by weather, especially the freezing and thawing of ice. Granite 'clitter' (displaced loose rocks) covers extensive areas.

Dartmoor is characterised by heather, gorse and invasive bracken in its drier areas and by mosses, cotton grass and reeds on its extensive bogs – all hardy flora able to survive the harsh climate in thin, acid, peaty soils. Due largely to clearance by prehistoric people (see page 14), high Dartmoor is virtually treeless apart from modern conifer plantations.

Haytor Rocks, are among Dartmoor's most popular destinations. They are also much used by rock climbers

However, three vestiges of ancient woodland survive of which Wistman's Wood is the most notable. In addition, the sheltered valleys leading away from the moor, such as the Dart, Plym, Bovey and Teign, are extensively wooded.

This is somewhat confusing, as large areas of mainly open moorland on high Dartmoor are marked on maps as 'Dartmoor Forest'. There is a reason: the whole of Devon was once 'Forest', that is, the king's hunting preserve, where game, notably deer, was protected by harsh laws. In 1204 the county was disafforested with the exceptions of Dartmoor and Exmoor. 'Dartmoor Forest' still belongs to the Duchy of Cornwall, and is the property of the monarch's eldest son.

Haytor Rocks (SX758771) are among Dartmoor's most impressive tors and finest viewpoints, with a panorama of eastern Dartmoor, the Teign Valley and on to the sea. The old quarries and unique granite tramway are another 'must' for visitors (see page 23). All can be readily accessed on foot from car parks on the Bovey Tracey-Widecombe road.

Wistman's Wood (SX612772) is one of three small remnants of the oak woods that covered all but the highest tors before clearances in the Neolithic and Bronze Ages. Gnarled and stunted oaks survive here because the rocks they grow among defend them from grazing animals. The mosses, lichens and liverworts which festoon the trees and the rocks below testify to the clean, moist air and are of exceptional botanical value – the wood is a National Nature Reserve.

Buckland Beacon (SX735731) at 380m offers a panorama which includes a ring of lofty tors, much of southern Dartmoor, the South Hams and on to the sea. Below are the thickly wooded valley of the Dart and Buckland church, both dwarfed by the vast landscape.

Combestone Tor

Rowtor seen from the East Okement car park

Combestone Tor (SX670718) is an attractive granite tor standing right beside the Holne to Hexworthy road. It offers spectacular views northwards. The stripes on the opposite hillside, Yartor, are Bronze Age reaves (see page 14).

Rowtor (SX595917) can be accessed from Okehampton on a road which passes Okehampton Camp. Rising rapidly to over 400m above sea level, this little used road gives a dramatic view of Dartmoor's highest tors, Yes Tor and High Willhays. At 619m and 621m they are just high enough to qualify as mountains. Rowtor is within the Okehampton military range. Please check it is open (page 32) before going there and do not enter if red flags are flying.

Picnic sites

Dartmoor is ideal for picnics. In addition to the reservoirs (pages 9-10) several picnic sites have car parks, toilets and picnic tables as marked on the OL28 map. All those listed below are in beautiful riverside locations by historic bridges and make good starting points for strolls or longer walks. Please remember not to feed the ponies, as this encourages them onto the roads, and do take litter home.

Bellever, 2km south of Postbridge (SX656772), see photo above. Clapper bridge, ford, stepping stones and turnpike trust bridge. Please note this is a Wildlife Action Zone, so avoid paddling in the river – it disturbs spawning fish.

New Bridge, Ashburton to Dartmeet road (SX711709). Walks by the river Dart. New Bridge is 15th century, though repaired many times – especially in recent years because of damage from HGVs.

Dartmeet, Ashburton to Princetown road (SX673733). Clapper bridge, turnpike trust bridge (1792) and stepping stones. There is quiet riverside north of the Badger's Holt tea rooms.

Hexworthy (Huccaby) Bridge, Holne to Hexworthy Cross road (SX659729). A favourite paddling spot.

Postbridge, Moretonhampstead to Princetown road (SX647788). One of Dartmoor's best medieval bridges (page 21). The car park houses an excellent information centre.

The Ring of Bells at North Bovey

The Rugglestone Inn, near Widecombe

Pubs

Dartmoor has a variety of beguiling and historic pubs, though they are not immune to the threat of closure which has hit many country inns recently. There are more good pubs than space to mention them. We have chosen a few for their history, quaintness and/or location:

Church House Inn, Holne (01364 631208)
Dartmoor Inn, Merrivale (01822 890340)
Forest Inn, Hexworthy (01364 631211)
Old Inn, Widecombe (01364 621207)
Rock Inn, Haytor (01364 661305)
Ring of Bells, North Bovey (01647 440375)
Rugglestone Inn, Widecombe (01364 621327)
Tavistock Inn, Poundsgate (01364 631251)
Warren House Inn, Postbridge (01822 880208)

Dartmoor's reservoirs

These man-made lakes are now so much a part of the landscape they appear natural and attract many visitors, especially walkers and trout fishermen. However, drowning farmland, moorland habitats and archaeological sites for water supply has long been a controversial issue. Eight reservoirs have been built within the National Park which, with its high rainfall and altitude, was an obvious place to site them. Meldon, the last, was approved in 1968, but plans for another Dartmoor reservoir were rejected in 1970.

The five reservoirs below are all in beautiful high moorland settings. Each provides a range of facilities, including parking, toilets, picnic areas, a circular walk and trout fishing. All of them are great starting points for moorland hikes. Contact South West Lakes Trust (01566 771930 www.swlakestrust.org.uk) for trout fishing details.

Avon Dam

The only way to reach Avon Dam (photo above) near South Brent is on foot, mountain bike or horseback. The most popular route is from the car park at Shipley Bridge, which has interesting remains from the peat and china clay industries. Take the gently graded and pretty riverside bridleway for 3 km to the dam. A circuit of the reservoir itself is very enjoyable, especially in droughts when many more prehistoric remains are revealed.

A lane circuits Burrator, which is surrounded by woods and granite tors. At 5.6km this makes a beautiful drive, or better a cycle ride or walk – it is fairly level by Dartmoor standards. Otherwise, park at Norsworthy Bridge, the quarry or the massive dam and enjoy the views, a picnic or an ice cream

Burrator

Drake's Leat, cut in 1590-91, was the first means of channelling Dartmoor water to Plymouth and remains important in moorland drainage. Drake's Leat was supplemented by Devonport Leat in 1793. However, the growing Victorian city needed much greater supplies, hence Burrator Reservoir near Yelverton, completed in 1898.

Meldon

Meldon's 23 hectares of open water just west of Okehampton are overlooked by Dartmoor's highest tors, High Willhays and Yes Tor. An attractive footpath leads along the north shore from the parking and picnic area and then onto northern Dartmoor's most rugged terrain.

Venford

Surrounded by trees, Venford is an attractive water. Built in 1907, it is reached via a lane between Holne and Hexworthy. A gentle footpath, ideal for families, circuits the reservoir and can be completed in 40 minutes.

Fernworthy

The beauty of Fernworthy can be enjoyed from the picnic area or by taking a walk around the reservoir. Fernworthy Forest contains prehistoric stone rows and circles, whilst the old bridges over the normally submerged South Teign reappear during droughts. There are two hides for birdwatching at the remote western end of the reservoir.

Truly grim and forbidding, and potentially dangerous, Fox Tor Mire inspired the 'Great Grimpen Mire' in Conan Doyle's 'Hound of the Baskervilles'

Dartmoor legends

Arthur Conan Doyle's *Hound of the Baskervilles* brought Dartmoor's rich heritage of legend to the attention of a wide audience far beyond Devon. Holmes' and Watson's most famous case is finally solved in a terrifying confrontation with the ferocious hound amid swirling Dartmoor mists at 'Grimpen Mire', based on Fox Tor Mire, 5km south of Princetown (SX620706).

The path across the desolate mire from the disused tin mine at Whiteworks (SX612710) cannot be recommended – it really is boggy and can be dangerous. However, a short walk will bring you to Nun's (otherwise Siward's) Cross at SX605699. This is at least 770 years old and, in common with many of Dartmoor's hundred plus stone crosses, served as a boundary and way marker, as well as the Christian symbol.

It bears a strong resemblance to Childe's Tomb across the mire at SX625703. Centuries ago, Childe the Hunter was caught in a terrible snow storm near here. His horse seemed to offer his only chance of survival, so he killed the beast and sheltered in its belly. Sadly, he froze to death anyway, but Dartmoor's legends are usually dark.

Disturbing tales surrounding the supposedly wicked Sir Richard Cabell of Buckfastleigh (who died in 1677) and his pack of hounds may have inspired Conan Doyle in creating the fictional Hugo Baskerville. Cabell's imposing tomb can be seen at Buckfastleigh church, which – fact sometimes being as dramatic as fiction – was largely destroyed by an arson attack in 1992.

With a little imagination, the frightening and deadly Baskerville hound with his glowing eyes can be conjured at Hound Tor near Manaton. Overlooking Hound Tor village (see page 18), these fantastic rock piles are said to be a pack of hounds turned to stone when their master, Bowerman, was punished for hunting with them over the moor on the Sabbath. Bowerman's Nose (SX741805), a nearby granite pile that certainly looks like a face, is reputedly Bowerman himself. In another version of the story, Bowerman mischievously disturbed a coven of witches and was petrified by them.

Crossing the moor was potentially dangerous. Vixen Tor (SX543743) near Merrivale is said to be the home of an evil witch, Vixana. She called down the notorious Dartmoor mists to lure travellers to their deaths in the nearby mire. One day a young man came to Vixana. She did not know he too had magic powers. He could see through mists and make himself invisible. As Vixana stood on her tor, waiting for the cold mist to clear, he crept up behind her and pushed her to a deserved doom in the mire.

Fresh flowers are always said to be found at Jay's Grave, where the body of a young woman was buried. According to Dartmoor writer Beatrice Chase, she was Mary Jay, born around 1790. Orphaned, she was apprenticed to a local farmer and is buried by the roadside at this lonely spot near Hound Tor at SX733799 because she committed suicide, probably after being jilted and left carrying a baby. (Suicides were not permitted burial in churchyards before 1823.)

Lightning struck Widecombe's church tower in 1638. It collapsed into the congregation and killed four people, as described by a poem in the church. Naturally, tales sprang up that the Devil was behind this terrible event. On the way to Widecombe to collect a debt from a wicked man (in another version to punish a boy sleeping during divine service), he is said to have visited the Tavistock Inn, Poundsgate. He left scorch marks on the bar and paid his bill with withered leaves.

The Moretonhampstead to Princetown road is said to be haunted between Postbridge and Two Bridges. Several motorcyclists have been killed on this stretch – their machines wrenched from their control by a mysterious pair of huge and hairy hands.

One of Britain's nine native breeds, the true Dartmoor is short (12.2 hands – 1.27m – or less) and stocky with a thick mane and tail to ward off winter rain and summer flies. Its winter coat is long and dense; its summer coat is seasonably shorter and sleeker

Ponies

Herds of ponies roam the moor all year round and help make Dartmoor the unique place it is. To survive the winters, they have to be hardy.

In the 19th and early 20th centuries cross-breeding diluted the Dartmoor pony stock and reduced their hardiness. Demand for working ponies almost ceased. All ponies are owned, but Dartmoor farmers had little incentive to keep them or check random breeding. Ponies attract no subsidies whereas sheep and cattle do – their numbers rose whilst the pony population plummeted from 30,000 in 1950 to around 3000 today. The future looked bleak, but in 1988 a scheme was launched to halt the decline and improve the quality of pony stock by running registered stallions with selected mares. It has had some success, further boosted by the recent work of the Dartmoor Pony Heritage Trust in preserving the breed.

The autumn 'drift', when the ponies are rounded up and herded off the moor by farmers, many mounted on horses and quad bikes, remains a great Dartmoor tradition and spectacle. Some animals are returned to the moor for breeding, others taken to local markets. Good tempered and intelligent, Dartmoors make excellent children's ponies and are increasingly used in carriage driving.

Their future is inextricably bound with Dartmoor's. Please help by not feeding them, which attracts them to roads, and by observing the 40mph speed limit. And do be aware that occasionally, if not given what they want, they may kick or bite!

The prehistoric period

Dartmoor is England's richest prehistoric landscape. The legacy of the past has survived better here than in the densely settled and farmed lowlands. In particular, most of Dartmoor has escaped ploughing, whilst its open nature – largely the result of prehistoric settlers burning the indigenous tree cover for grazing and crops – makes finding prehistoric remains much easier – especially during the winter and spring, before the bracken grows.

Over 5000 'hut circles' (the foundations of prehistoric buildings, not all of them houses) have been recorded on Dartmoor, as well as 18 stone circles and at least 75 stone rows. There are more and longer stone rows on Dartmoor than anywhere else in Britain, varying from a few metres to over 3km in length, as well as impressive standing stones, burial chambers and mounds. A remarkable 400km of Early Bronze Age 'reaves' survive too. Ruler-straight boundaries, they mark out the best preserved prehistoric field systems in Britain, possibly in Europe.

Merrivale

Merrivale has Dartmoor's most accessible concentration of antiquities. There is a car park 500m east of the Dartmoor Inn at SX554750 on the Two Bridges/Tavistock road. Two double stone rows over 200m long and each with a standing stone, are easily found. With seven cairns, the foundations of a partially enclosed round house settlement and a stone circle, the immediate area is well worth exploring and the setting superb.

Whilst the stone rows may date from around 2000 BC (Early Bronze Age), the other features may be of similar age or slightly later, and the hut circles are tentatively dated to 1500 BC – possibly after the stone rows had gone out of use.

Shovel Down

Shovel Down near Teigncombe on the north-eastern side of Dartmoor has another rich concentration of prehistoric remains. The Shovel Down complex includes three double stone rows which meet at a retaining circle. The Long Stone, 3.2 m high and later utilised as a boundary marker, was associated with these. So too was 'Three Boys', now only one extant stone, which probably represents the large stones often found at the end of a row. There is a nearby Bronze Age field system, centred on Kes Tor, which is later than the ceremonial complex.

Park near Batworthy, at the end of the lane (SX662864). This is just beyond the Round Pound (SX664868), a hut 11 m in diameter within a 33 m outer wall. Excavations suggest the Round Pound was abandoned, then reused for metalworking during the Iron Age and again during the medieval period.

Above left: One of the double stone rows at Merrivale

Right: The Round Pound lies just to the right of the tree. Leading towards it are the walls of a Bronze Age drove road: for thousands of years, animals were led up to the moor for summer grazing

Scorhill Stone Circle

A 1km walk north from the Shovel Down complex leads to two clapper bridges at Teign-e-ver, with its waterfalls and boulders, including the famous 'Tolmen' or holed stone, just downstream of the clapper. Scorhill Circle is approximately 500m further north at SX655874. Most of the stones are of modest size, but the tallest is a dignified 2.4m tall and the circle is 27m in diameter. Scorhill is as time has left it, unlike some other Dartmoor circles where zealous Victorian antiquarians re-erected fallen stones.

There has been much debate about whether circles such as this (and associated stone rows) were erected to calculate time and the seasons by aligning the stones with the sun and the stars. This appears very possible. However, a working calendar could be made by erecting a circle of sticks, thus saving thousands of man hours erecting heavy stones, some of which weigh several tons. Clearly, powerful ritual or religious motives also drove prehistoric man to build features such as Scorhill Circle, but exactly what they were will probably always remain a mystery.

Grimspound

Grimspound (SX701809) is Dartmoor's most impressive prehistoric site and something no visitor should miss. A high double-walled enclosure of 1.6ha protecting 24 hut circles makes it look like a fort at first glance, but its sheltered position in the Challacombe valley would have been of little defensive worth, being easy to attack from high ground. It was probably built as a pound to keep domestic animals in and predators such as wolves and foxes out.

Enter Grimspound and, with a little imagination, step back into the Bronze Age when it was built and sheltered a community of perhaps fifty people, who herded sheep and cattle, grew crops (probably beans and oats) and hunted abundant game. The Dartmoor Exploration Committee restored the paved entrance to the pound in the late 19th century and re-erected one hut wall to its original height. They also re-established the central bearing stone for the roof support, the hearth and the doorway.

Opposite Grimspound are the deep gullies dug by tin miners at Headland Warren and the field patterns created by medieval farmers at Challacombe village 1km south.

Climb Hameldown for a magnificent Dartmoor panorama and an aerial view of Grimspound that shows its shape, size and purpose to full advantage.

Above: The Hound Tor medieval hamlet
Opposite: Hutholes medieval hamlet

The medieval period

Dartmoor tin and the Stannaries

The earliest surviving reference to Devon's tin industry was made in 1156. As deposits of tin-bearing rocks and gravels from rivers were exhausted, miners dug pits and gullies in pursuit of tin lodes. Many parts of Dartmoor are scarred by this work; the hillside at Challacombe opposite Grimspound (page 17) is a prime example. At a later period, deep shafts were dug as at Vitifer and Birch Tor (page 22).

Tin ore was broken down on site in a crazing mill, much as corn is ground. Later, more efficient water-driven 'stamps' were introduced. Water also drove the bellows in peat-fired smelting furnaces known as 'blowing houses', examples of which are found at Merrivale (SX 553763), Black Tor Falls (SX 575716) and elsewhere. Dartmoor's abundant rainfall, channelled through many leats that still criss-cross the moor, drove the mining industry and remained important even in the age of steam, since there was no convenient source of coal. As an integral part of the moor's drainage, leats still serve a useful purpose.

Until 1838 all smelted tin was, by law, taken to one of Dartmoor's four Stannary towns – Chagford, Plympton, Ashburton and Tavistock – for assay, tax and sale. Legally processed ingots were 'coigned' (the corners cut) and stamped, but some tin was inevitably smuggled out. Each stannary town had jurisdiction over a sector of Dartmoor.

The first Warden of the Stannaries was appointed in 1198. Wardens continued to regulate tinning until the 19th century. Between 1494 and 1730 they convoked Tinners' Parliaments at Crockern Tor where the bounds of the four Stannaries met. Stannary Law had remarkable force. Tinners were exempt from prosecution in any court but their own Stannary courts, except in cases of life, limb and freehold. They were also exempt from ordinary taxation and from all tolls in towns, fairs and markets.

Hound Tor and Hutholes medieval hamlets

In the early medieval period there was great population expansion. Many new settlements were created and fields enclosed, even on the more sheltered slopes of Dartmoor. However, with the Black Death of 1348-9 – a devastating plague which, it is estimated, killed half the people in Europe – countless farms and villages on marginal land were abandoned, including 130 on Dartmoor alone.

Hound Tor village (600m SE of the car park at SX746788) and Hutholes near Widecombe (SX702759) are both intriguing examples

A surviving longhouse, Middle Bonehill near Widecombe

of abandoned settlements. Excavated and now open to the public, they show substantial granite foundations. The most impressive are the longhouses which were characteristic of upland Britain, not least medieval Dartmoor.

In a longhouse people and their animals lived under one roof and shared the same entrance. A cross passage separated the human quarters – usually one or two ground floor chambers open to the roof in medieval times – from the shippon. Here, the animals were sheltered, their body heat helping to warm the house.

As can be seen, longhouses followed the contours of the land, with the shippon facing downhill. A central drain then allowed animal waste to flow downhill. Exploring Hound Tor or Hutholes, it is easy to imagine the scene, the farmer driving his animals in from the little walled fields around and the acrid smoke drifting slowly up from the open hearth in the living chamber through the thatched roof.

Such sophistications as chimneys, second storeys and separate entrances for people were later additions to the primitive medieval ground plan. Mainly added in the 16th and 17th centuries as rising prosperity allowed, they must have improved conditions immensely. Over one hundred inhabited longhouses survive on Dartmoor, including some very handsome buildings with datestones over carved porches. Most of the surviving longhouses are in more sheltered spots than Hound Tor or Hutholes.

20

The clapper bridge at Postbridge

River crossings on Dartmoor gradually developed to meet changing needs. Wet, slippery, sometimes dangerous or impassable, fords and stepping stones were replaced by clapper bridges on the more frequently used routes. At several river crossings, including Dartmeet (page 7) and Two Bridges two or more bridges can be seen together. The evolution is best seen at Bellever on the East Dart (page 7) with a ford, stepping stones and two later bridges.

Standing beside an arched turnpike trust bridge of the 1770s, built for the newly re-constructed Exeter to Tavistock post-road, Postbridge is the most impressive of Dartmoor's many clapper bridges, with a span of 13 m and exceptionally tall stone piers.

Clappers are simple structures of flat stone slabs, ranging from a single span over moorland streams to two or three spans on wider rivers. They are usually impossible to date accurately, but some, including Postbridge, may have originated during the early medieval expansion of Dartmoor settlement. However, Dartmoor rivers can rise swiftly and violently, so most bridges have been repaired and reconstructed several times over the centuries. It is known of Postbridge that a young farmer threw down the central slab in 1825 to create a duck pond, but it was replaced in 1880.

Industrial remains

Powdermills

The Powder Mills, a Victorian gunpowder factory by the Postbridge-Two Bridges road at SX626769, is one of Dartmoor's most interesting industrial ruins. The old school cum chapel is now a studio pottery, where Joss Hibbs makes her distinctive wood-fired pots entirely from Dartmoor materials. A shop selling various local crafts, a café and a bunkhouse are on the site, and a few cottages remain.

The Powder Mills were sited in this lonely spot for good reasons. Making 'black powder' was dangerous – despite many precautions, including a ban on steel tools and hobnailed boots, there were several explosions. One in 1857 killed two men and seriously injured a third. Anticipating accidents, George Frean, who founded the Powder Mills in 1844, built the stores and workshops with very thick stone walls and light wooden roofs to direct the explosions upwards.

Despite its remoteness, the site was close to Dartmoor's mines and quarries, ready markets for its black powder. It also stands by the Cherrybrook. The water was run through three linked waterwheels by leats, providing cheap (and safe) power to run the mills and hydraulic presses. These remain as ruins, but the proving mortar, in which gunpowder was tested by firing a 68lb (31kg) ball over a measured distance, remains in serviceable condition by the drive. It and Powdermills were rendered obsolete by the invention of dynamite in the late 19th century.

Vitifer and Birch Tor mines

Dartmoor was intensively exploited for minerals, especially tin, from at least medieval times until the early 20th century. The adjoining

A strange landscape of deep gullies at Vitifer Mine. Care is needed when exploring these sites, especially if you have children or dogs with you

This Haytor quarry is always picturesque, but never more so than this

Vitifer and Birch Tor mines form the densest concentration of workings. They lie just south of the B3212 between Bennett's Cross (one of the most striking of Dartmoor's 130 ancient crosses) and the Warren House Inn – which was built in 1845 and named after the artificial rabbit warrens dug to keep miners in meat.

At their peak in 1864 the Vitifer/Birch Tor mines employed 150 people. Mining ceased by the Second World War, when the area was disturbed by bomb disposal work. Paths give access to Vitifer and Birch Tor which, like all former industrial sites, are potentially hazardous and must be explored carefully.

The ground is deeply pitted with gullies, where lodes were dug out from the surface from early times, and also with shafts from 18th and 19th century mines. There are numerous spoil heaps and wheelpits which powered the mines. Many mine buildings survive as foundations, including dressing floors, carpenters' and blacksmiths' shops, a miners' 'dry', dormitory, kitchen, canteen and mine captain's house.

Haytor quarries and granite tramway

Dartmoor granite was quarried from around 1780. Like hard rock mining, the industry reached peak production in the 19th century and then declined in the face of competition from cheaper producers.

Granite was last quarried in the 1990s, at Merrivale. Haytor's quarries are among the best known. They supplied stone for the old London Bridge and the British Museum Library and were served by a tramway with granite rails.

Effectively Devon's first railway, the tramway used granite rails with a raised edge and horse-drawn wagons without flanged wheels. Each wagon could carry up to three tonnes of stone from the five quarries on Haytor Down. Apart from a short section uphill from Holwell Quarry, it was downhill 394m all the way to waiting barges on the canal at Teigngrace, 13.6km distant. The barges took the granite onward to ships at Teignmouth.

Although the quarries have not been worked since 1919, when stone was cut for Exeter's war memorial, long sections of the tramway can be traced on foot, especially around Haytor Rocks. Leave your car in the lower Haytor car park by the information centre. Follow the well beaten path 600m north to the first of the quarries. Now partly filled with water, the quarry is a charming and sheltered spot with some machinery, including a rusted winch, still in place. The tramway can be followed from the quarry entrance for 300m to a junction. From that point it can be followed right or (better) left, where the best preserved sections lead to Holwell quarries.

Princetown and the Prison

Princetown is surprisingly modern, and the prison began as a business enterprise. Building of the village was begun in 1785 by Sir Thomas Tyrwhitt, who named it (rather sycophantically) after his friend, the Prince of Wales, the future George IV. He also drained the area, built a fine house for himself at Tor Royal and planned some hopelessly optimistic agricultural projects.

War with Napoleon's France produced more prisoners of war than British prisons and prison hulks, many moored in Plymouth Sound, could cope with. Tyrwhitt responded by building Princetown Prison between 1806 and 1809. Following the fashion of the day, the granite prison blocks were laid out like the spokes of a wheel. As cheap labour in Tyrwhitt's quarries and road building schemes, or building Princetown church, the 8000 French prisoners of war brought some prosperity to Dartmoor, whilst French officers with private means boarded in Dartmoor towns on their parole (word of honour). The War of 1812 brought an additional 1700 American prisoners.

However, most prisoners suffered a miserable existence. Violence and disease were rife and food was short. Between 1809 and 1816 1470 prisoners died, most in the prime of life.

Peace with France and America was bad news for Tyrwhitt.

25

The trackbed of the Plymouth & Dartmoor Railway makes ideal level walking, and can be followed west from Princetown. You will rarely find a vehicle on it, but here a Dartmoor farmer was visiting his flock of sheep

Tyrwhitt's solution was to build Devon's first iron railway, the Plymouth & Dartmoor. Originally a horse-drawn tramway, serving Swell Tor and Foggintor quarries, it was extended to Princetown in 1826. Re-launched in 1883, it carried traffic until 1956.

Meanwhile, the prison was empty. When Australia refused to accept any more British convicts in 1850, some of the toughest were sent to Dartmoor and the prison farm was established in 1852. For a brief period during the First World War the convicts were moved out (some were drafted into the armed forces) and conscientious objectors moved in.

A punitive regime of hard discipline, hard labour and meagre diet prevailed until recent times. Dartmoor became a 'Category C' prison in 2001 and no longer houses high risk prisoners. The emphasis today is on education and rehabilitation. The prison's grim history can be studied at the Prison Heritage Centre (page 30). Princetown's other main point of interest is the High Moorland Visitor Centre (page 30), plus its shops, cafés and pubs. Ask for Dartmoor or Jail ales, brewed in Princetown.

Villages

Widecombe-in-the-Moor

Nestling beneath high rocky tors in the Webburn valley, this beautiful granite village has a tree-shaded green, cafés and gift shops and a church of exceptional dignity. Crowned with a 41 m tall tower, the 'cathedral of the moor' was enlarged in the 15th and 16th centuries with profits from tinning. In 1638, it was struck by lightning, killing four people and injuring 62, as verses in the north aisle recall (see page 12).

The song 'Widecombe Fair' has made the village famous far beyond Devon. Full of wry country humour, it tells how Uncle Tom Cobley and his six friends rode to Widecombe Fair on the back of an old grey mare. Held every September, the fair features pony, sheep and cattle shows, races, craft demonstrations and sideshows. Less well-known, the village market is a great place to buy local produce and is held in the Church House, usually on the fourth Saturday of each month.

Otherwise, the 16th century Church House serves as a National Trust shop and local information centre plus village hall. As well as its unique loggia on granite posts, it houses a massive pair of bellows, a cruck-beamed roof and the village stocks.

Widecombe's Old Inn is said to be 14th century. It has three good stone fireplaces, period photographs and oil paintings. More photographs of the Fair and the local hunt can be seen at the Rugglestone, a friendly locals' pub 1km away.

Buckland-in-the-Moor – sheltered by tall beeches, the pretty moorstone church has a richly carved and painted rood-screen, whilst the tower clock is marked with the letters MY DEAR MOTHER instead of the usual numerals

Buckland-in-the-Moor

Granite cottages, dry stone walls and thatched roofs combine to make a harmony of warm grey tones and lush vegetation.

North Bovey

Cob and thatch cottages circle the village green with its stone cross and iron pump. Many of the village forefathers sleep under carved floor slabs in North Bovey's typically Devonian 15th century granite church, which has wagon roofs with carved bosses and a carved rood-screen. The Ring of Bells pub reputedly began as a lodging house for masons building the church. Later it became a farmhouse and then an inn. It is a fascinating building with thick granite walls, low ceilings, bread oven and thatched roof.

Walking on Dartmoor

Dartmoor provides superb walking. In addition to 723 km (449 miles) of public rights of way, a large part of the moor – over 35,000 hectares – is open access. Guided walks are a great way to start. DNPA offers a programme of over 400 walks led by expert guides to suit all levels of fitness and a wide variety of interests. There's a modest fee, but that's waived if you arrive by public transport. Alternatively, buy a walks book (see page 32), a compass and the Ordnance Survey OL28 map, which shows rights of way and open access areas.

Walking on Dartmoor is safe and trouble-free, so long as you're prepared. Good walking boots and suitable clothing are essential. Dartmoor weather can change suddenly, thus waterproofs and an extra layer of clothing are as vital as ample drinking water and a comfortable rucksack. Many, including me, add a walking stick, mobile phone and food.

Check first if you want to enter the military ranges on the remoter northern parts of Dartmoor (see page 32 for details). The ranges are marked on Ordnance Survey Explorer OL28 map and on the ground by a series of red and white posts. Do not enter when the red flags are flying. Normally, there is no live firing at weekends and during the main holiday periods. Leave any strange objects in case they are unexploded ordnance and contact the police, 08452 777444, or Commandant, 01837 650010.

What to do if it rains

Inevitably, rain comes often to Dartmoor. It's always a good idea to have waterproofs handy for any Dartmoor trip, but we've listed a range of indoor visits for those days when the heavens open. Including the fringes of the moor, there's a good choice of activities, some of which are described in greater detail in our companion guide, *Dartmoor with Your Kids*. Information about these places can date, so you may want to check before visiting.

The High Moorland Visitor Centre, Princetown (01822 890414) is open daily year round (save Christmas and one week in March) with free admission. Visitors can watch films about Dartmoor, listen to oral history on CD, and enjoy a rolling programme featuring local photography and painting. Interpretive displays aided by touch screen computers bring Dartmoor's landscape, wildlife, heritage and history vividly to life. Helpful staff provide advice and information, plus a range of Dartmoor maps and books. Opposite is the **Duchy Centre for Creativity** (01822 890828), home to a variety of arts and crafts.

Princetown is centred on its prison. **Dartmoor Prison Heritage Centre**, Princetown (01822 322130) offers a fascinating insight into its history from its opening for prisoners of war in 1809 to the present.

Dingles Fairground Heritage Centre, Lifton (01566 783425) lies west of Dartmoor just off the A30 and is clearly signed. Housing the national fairground collection, including vintage vehicles and engineering plus stunning period artwork, it makes a unique diversion and offers a programme of special events, plus a gift shop and café.

Recently refurbished, the **Museum of Dartmoor Life**, Okehampton (01837 52295) provides a good introduction to local history. Housed in a 19th century mill with a working waterwheel, it has a range of interactive exhibits. Other museums include **Bovey Heritage Centre** (01626 834331), **Ashburton Museum** (01364 652698) and **Tavistock Museum** (01822 612546).

Castle Drogo (National Trust), Drewsteignton, towers over the spectacular Teign Gorge and enjoys superb Dartmoor views. England's newest castle (1930!) is furnished with a variety of antiques. Special events are often offered (01647 433306 for details and opening times). If the weather lifts, try the attractive gardens or explore the gorge and riverbank on foot.

Also National Trust are **Finch Foundry**, Sticklepath (01837 840046), a water powered forge in working order with three waterwheels, and **Buckland Abbey**, Buckland Monachorum. Owned successively by the Elizabethan seafarers Drake and Grenville, the Abbey has permanent exhibitions about them. There is also a huge tithe barn, craft workshops and a strong events programme (details 01822 853607), plus an Elizabethan garden and extensive grounds.

Buckfast Abbey (01364 645550), rebuilt by a small dedicated team of monks during the late 19th and early 20th centuries on the foundations of the ruined medieval abbey, is famed for its 8 m stained glass window. It also has shops and a restaurant.

Nearby is the **South Devon Railway** (01364 642338), a restored steam railway following the beautiful Dart Valley to historic Totnes.

Re-opened in 2009, the **Dartmoor Railway** (01837 55164) is part of the former Southern Railway line from London Waterloo to Plymouth. From Okehampton station, restored in full period style, there are scenic rides to Meldon Viaduct and up the line to Sampford Courtenay and Yeoford.

Dartmoor Zoological Park, Sparkwell (01752 837645) is home to over 200 animals from stick insects to bears and lions. **Buckfastleigh Butterflies and Dartmoor Otters** (01364 642916) houses vivid butterflies from around the world and otters at play – feeding times are especially lively.

Tavistock has a range of independent shops and a large indoor pannier market, open Tuesdays to Saturdays and selling crafts, books, food, clothing and much more.

Bargain hunters will be delighted with **Trago Mills**, near Newton Abbot, a shopping mall that offers a huge range of discounted goods from carpets to paperclips, plus a large variety of entertainments, from go-karts and trampolines to a narrow gauge railway.

The Devon Guild of Craftsmen, Bovey Tracey (01626 832223) is both a gallery and a shop, with the best of Devon's arts and crafts on view, and free entry.

Also free at Bovey Tracey, **The House of Marbles** (01626 835358) combines the functions of toy shop, marble museum and glass blowing workshop, with regular displays.

Further south, **The Cider Press**, Dartington (01803 847500), has a range of craft outlets and other interesting shops.

Further information

The Ordnance Survey map Explorer OL28 provides a wealth of detail with easily read symbols. Dartmoor National Park Authority (01626 832093) www.dartmoor-npa.gov.uk is a prime source of information and runs local centres around the moor:

High Moorland Visitor Centre, Princetown (01822 890414)
Postbridge (01822 880272)
Haytor (01364 661520)

There are also excellent Information Centres at

Ashburton (01364 653426)
Bovey Tracey (01626 832047)
Buckfastleigh (01364 644522)
Ivybridge (01752 897035)
Moretonhampstead (01647 440043)
Okehampton (01837 53020)
Tavistock (01822 612938)

There is a particularly informative website giving information about aspects of the moor: www.virtuallydartmoor.org.uk

Finally, you can check first if you want to enter the military ranges on the remoter northern parts of Dartmoor by calling:
Freephone 0800 458 4868 www.dartmoor-ranges.co.uk *or*
DNPA 01626 832093 www.dartmoor-npa.gov.uk

Bossiney walks books for Dartmoor
Really Short Walks – North Dartmoor (3-5km)
Really Short Walks – South Dartmoor (3-5km)
Shortish Walks on Dartmoor (5-8km)
North Dartmoor Pub Walks (8-13km)
South Dartmoor Pub Walks (8-13km)
Walks on High Dartmoor (7-20km)

Other Bossiney books about Dartmoor
Dartmoor with Your Kids
Ancient Dartmoor
Medieval Dartmoor
The Making of Modern Dartmoor
Ponies on Dartmoor
Cycle Rides South-West – Dartmoor